"Don't just read this book. Come back to it again and again. Settle into its comforting ideas like you would your favorite chair."
　H. Joseph Jones, manager
　External Affairs, Appalachian Power

"Instant Stress Busters looks great! I read it and already feel at ease :) I love the format—I love the Why It Works segments."
　Kathryn Lester, MBA, financial advisor

"Thank you, Aila! Your 34 Instant Stress-Busters is timely and on target. Stress is so rampant these days and millions can benefit from your book and experience. BRAVO!"
　Joel Fellman, senior vice president, www.altMD.com

"With her wonderfully warm writing style, Aila offers a guide to live by. This marvelous book is filled with simple yet profoundly effective stress release techniques. If you're ready to have a peaceful and positively empowered life, read and live this book!"
　Joan Shannon, MS, teacher, coach and entrepreneur

"I LOVE IT! You certainly put yourself into this work of love."
　Margaret D. Valderrey, MSN, RN, CNS, director
　Mental Health and Pharmacy Education,
　Charlotte AHEC / Regional Education Services

"34 Instant Stress-Busters is a great source of information that people can use bit by bit in our busy life."
　Sally Miller, nutritionist, www.eatsofeden.com

www.ailaspeaks.com

Quick Tips to De-Stress Fast
with No Extra Time or Money

by Aila Accad, RN, MSN

www.ailaspeaks.com

flowingowlpress

Flowing Owl Press
1800 Woodvale Drive
Charleston, WV 25314

Printed in the United States of America

Library of Congress Control Number: 2009928970
ISBN 978-0-9840689-0-6-0

Edited by Carol Melling

Cover Graphics and Composition – Ron Keeling
Printed by The Printing Press, LTD., Charleston, WV

For information about special discounts
and bulk purchases, please contact:

LifeQuest International, LLC at 304-344-9131

www.ailaspeaks.com

This book is dedicated to my favorite stress-busters
my grandchildren

Martina, Eden, Aillea and Alfred

Acknowledgements

I am grateful to all the people who ceaselessly support and encourage my growth and sharing of wisdom

Especially
Joan Shannon, Bob Cuccioli, JR Keener, Kathy Lester, Julia Sadd, Barbie Dallman, Donna Hamra, Harry Fini, My Diamond Heart family and my amazing clients.

My heartfelt thanks go to the people who generously shared their editing and publishing talents

Especially
Carol Melling, Mary Angel & Ron Keeling

CONTENTS

Introduction

As a registered nurse, I am intimately aware of how the pressures and strains of life take their toll, not only on your body but on all areas of your life.

I also know that even though the outer world throws many stressors your way, like time pressures, technology, change, work, finances, relationships and more, you can reclaim control of the impact stress has on you.

Stress triggers responses in the body—blood pressure-raising, heart-racing, head-aching, muscle-tensing, stomach-churning kinds of responses. When these responses continue for long periods without relief, they eventually become chronic conditions, illness and disease.

This quick tip book contains proven ways to reclaim control over stress so you can inexpensively reduce your stress and quickly provide your body, mind, emotions, spirit and relationships the temporary relief so desperately needed. Practiced over time, these techniques will help you achieve permanent stress relief.

Even though I have divided the Quick Tips into separate chapter headings of Body, Mind, Emotions, Spirit and Relationships to indicate the primary focus of the tip, this is not the way de-stressing works. We are whole and complete beings who do not have parts that function separately from one another. Each one of these de-stress tips affects your total being for the better.

So begin your personal de-stressing plan with any tip in the book. Pick the tips that appeal to you the most or seem easiest for you to integrate into your day.

You can't get rid of the craziness that happens in life, but you can change your perspective on and reactions to what happens. By doing this, you regain power over your health, energy and life enjoyment.

My intention in writing this book is to give you quick stress-busting techniques that you can use immediately to release stress and allow more ease and joy into your life.

Why not start with one Quick Tip right now, then add more over time to develop a daily de-stress plan that is perfect for you?

My sincere desire is that you experience less stress and more health, happiness and peace in your life.

Warm :)))

Aila

Chapter 1

How to Use This Book

Keep It Simple.

Small Daily Steps
Apply these stress-busters regularly throughout the day as you notice stress building up. Small changes at regular intervals work best.

Changing your stress habit patterns takes time. DO NOT discourage yourself by attempting too many changes at once. Pick the tips you like best and implement them one or two at a time for a week or more until they feel like a comfortable part of your daily routine.

Over time, you will find yourself generally less stressed in a way that feels completely natural to you!

Why It Works
Included with each tip is an explanation of "why it works." These are suggestions for integrating the tip into your day and principles that can help you to expand this short list of strategies with ideas of your own.

Let Go of Perfection
Feel free to adapt the tips to fit your style and schedule. There is no one perfect way to implement these tips. Be open to discover what works for you. Play with the ideas and adapt them to free your life force energy by reducing your stress.

Daily/Weekly Plan
Take time to set a plan for how you will integrate a tip or two each week. You will find a planner to use at the end

of each major chapter. Make copies of the planner so you can use it over again for new tips that you want to integrate into your life.

Observe and adjust the plan to fit your lifestyle and needs. Keep moving forward and enjoy progress rather than trying to achieve perfection.

De-Stress Together
Do you know someone else who also wants to de-stress? Ask that person to read this book too. Then support each other in making changes successfully together.

You might even plan to de-stress as a friendship, family or work group. The more people choose to de-stress around you, the more quickly you will all succeed at being freer, happier and more productive.

Additional Resources
I've listed some of my favorite supportive resources for you in Chapter 10.

In addition, I'm including a special gift for you here, my downloadable guided meditation, "Relaxing Your Body and Mind." You will find that this powerfully relaxing voice track with its soothing original musical background is perfect for resting deeply before bed or anytime. Go to the following web page to download the MP3 to your computer or ipod: http://www.ailaspeaks.com/book-bonus-MP3.html.

Personal one-to-one or group coaching by phone can be a powerful resource for integrating these tips and more.

You can learn more about my specialized coaching programs at www.ailaspeaks.com/coaching.html.

Chapter 2

A Little HerStory

I first remember feeling hopelessly stressed at the age of nine. Sitting on the edge of my bed one night, I cried out, "Holy Spirit, either tell me why I am here or take me back!"

I felt a sense of peace flow through my body. At that

moment I knew in my heart that one day I would have an answer.

That assurance set me on a life quest to explore the answer to life's apparent illogical insanity and the reason for my existence in it.

I learned a lot through books, classes and various spiritual and psychological paths. This resulted in becoming a very knowledgeable expert on the subject of STRESS. As a nurse, teacher and trainer, I am constantly consulted by people about their stressful lives. At that time, I could share what I learned intellectually even though my core stress was still present.

Then, on my birthday, October 6, 1987, I had a "moment of truth," an awakening.

By October each year, my "to-do" list was out of control. I said "Yes" to what everyone needed from me. I never considered how unrealistic my expectation was that I could fulfill all those demands.

That year I sat on the sofa, pulled the cover over my head and cried. I wanted to disappear. I wasn't suicidal, just overwhelmed. I wanted to go away for three months and start over again with a clean slate.

I wondered, "What if I had a heart attack and died right now? Who would do all of this?" The answers were life-changing!

My mind pictured how others would pick up the essential jobs. My organized ten-year-old daughter, who enjoys cooking, would prepare dinner. My twelve-year-old son would help with laundry and other tasks. My husband would grocery shop and deal with school issues, but probably not bake brownies and cupcakes.

No one else would do many of the tasks I was doing. I had to ask myself, "Why am I doing them?" The answer to this question was most revealing.

I began to realize that most of my "to-dos" were not mine at all. Most of them came from others' "to-do" lists, starting with mom and dad. I never re-evaluated my list or took anything off when I added something new. I never actually wrote my list. It was all in my head, heart and cellular memory!

I also realized that my orientation to taking care of everyone and everything by myself started very early in life. By three, I was mom's helper with a new baby. I was continuously employed by others, starting with baby-sitting from the age of ten, through college and marriage, then self-employed after the kids came along.

Nursing school education reinforced and capitalized on my strengths and capacity for large responsibility. By the time

I married and started my family, the habit of doing everything perfectly and alone was well ingrained and unquestioned.

From that day of awakening forward, my life quest took a turn toward depth. Nothing was too sacred to question. All that I knew intellectually I either validated experientially or released through an intensive self-discovery process.

Today, I not only "know," "understand" and "teach" about stress, I "live" a de-stressed and happy life.

I am delighted to be able to offer you books, programs, coaching and products that quickly and effectively simplify the process of de-stressing with far less time and financial investment than I spent.

You will find the growing list of resources available to support your journey in Chapter 10.

Chapter 3

What Is Stress?

There are two kinds of stress, distress and eustress. Distress is the kind that results in deterioration of your system. Eustress is the kind that supports your life force energy and helps you feel alive and productive.

The purpose of this book is to help you quickly reduce your Distress so you can enhance your life by releasing the Eustress or energy that supports your passion and goals.

The word "stress" in this book refers to distress.

Stanford Medical School and the World Health Organization agree that stress causes 85-95% of all illness and disease.

What is stress?

On a primitive level, you have protective fight, flight and freeze responses that effectively help you to deal with immediate or perceived threats to survival. When you engage these responses for long periods without rest, the body deteriorates. Chronic stress shuts down the immune system, resulting in chronic illness.

Being on "red alert" for long periods in this high-pressure culture is the norm for most people. So are fatigue, irritability, autoimmune syndromes like fibromyalgia and chronic fatigue, addictions, obesity and chronic disease.

The answer to chronic stress is awareness of the automatic protective process of shutdown and attention to your basic needs. What are those basic needs?

Your body needs five things to stay well – food (nutrition), air, water, sun and rest. Your mind needs a sense of control. Your emotions need expression and attention. Your spirit needs freedom to expand and move. Your relationships need autonomy and respect.

When you do not have what you need in these areas, stress creates the pressure to get what you need. When you don't respond appropriately to the pressure, it continues to build until your system literally shuts down.

The tips in this book are great ways to de-stress quickly by giving yourself what you need again, starting right now!

Stress Stats

The U.S. Bureau of Labor estimates stress costs U.S. businesses $300 billion annually in lost productivity, absenteeism, accidents, employee turnover and medical costs.

"Attitudes In The American Workplace VI" Gallup Poll found that:
- *80% of workers feel stress on the job and nearly half say they need help in learning how to manage stress.*
- *42% say their coworkers need such help.*
- *14% felt like striking a coworker in the past year, but didn't.*
- *25% felt like screaming or shouting because of job stress.*
- *10% are concerned about an individual at work they fear could become violent.*
- *9% are aware of an assault or violent act in their workplace.*
- *18% had experienced some sort of threat or verbal intimidation in the past year.*

Centers for Disease Control and Prevention reports that up to 90 percent of the doctor visits in the USA may be triggered by a stress-related illness.

Roper Starch Worldwide survey of 30,000 people between the ages of 13 and 65 in 30 countries showed:
- *Women who work full-time and have children under the age of 13 report the greatest stress worldwide.*
- *Nearly one in four mothers who work full-time and have children under 13 feel feel stress almost every day.*

Chapter 4

De-Stress Your Body

The Essentials for Life

Your body's needs are simple, which makes this a great place to start de-stressing. The following Quick Tips address your body's basic needs for air, water, food, sun and rest.

Most of our food today does not have adequate natural nutrition. Modern convenience has led to soil depletion, processing, irradiation, microwaving and chemical additives to food. You cannot eat enough modern food to get the nutrition your cells need and want. This is part of the reason we are overly hungry and eat to obesity.

We live and work in sealed environments, breathing re-circulated air for long periods. Much of our air and water contains chemicals and we are supposed to stay out of the sun or add chemical barriers to our skin to protect us from the vital rays we need.

Working long hours in sedentary jobs, watching television and overstimulating our system with caffeine, sugar and other chemicals can create sleep deprivation and fatigue.

Living in the world requires attention and conscious choice to give your body what it needs to stay well. Your body is amazing! It has its own self-repair mechanisms and does not require perfect resources to be well. Movement in the right direction will do wonders.

Choose raw, organic, locally grown nutrition when possible. Breathe tree-cleansed air when possible. Take in ten minutes of sun early in the morning or later in the afternoon when possible. Move and stretch a little more during the day. Your body can recover quickly with these Quick Tips.

Quick Tip # 1 ~ Take a Deep Breath

Take a deep breath, center yourself and smile. Breathing relaxes and restores both body and mind.

When your body is under stress, breathing becomes shallow. You might even notice that you hold your breath.

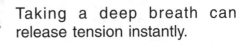

Taking a deep breath can release tension instantly.

Oxygen immediately starts to flow to the cells. Energy is free to move throughout your body again.

As you take a deep breath, take it all the way into every cell of your body. Feel your belly expand. When you let it out, let it out with a sound – Ahhhhh.

Allow your shoulders to drop and feel relaxation move through your body. Smile.

Test this for yourself: Notice how you are breathing when you are in a meeting, confronted with a challenge or nervously anticipating something. Immediately take a deep breath, let it out and notice how you feel again.

You will feel not only more relaxed but also more energized. Your brain gets more oxygen to think clearly and energy flows instead of being constricted or stuck.

This is the simplest, quickest and most useful thing to do to reduce stress continuously throughout the day.

—Why It Works—

When the body stresses, breathing becomes shallow. Talking a deep breath gives your cells the oxygen they need. The body relaxes and the mind is sharper.

When you take that breath deep into the pelvic floor, you will find you stand up straighter and feel more centered and balanced. Standing strong and in charge of your next step feels great, so smile!

When you smile, you actually feel better. Smiling is a physical cue indicating you are happy, so endorphins start to flow. A genuine smile cues everyone around you, too. You may also find that others respond better to you.

Quick Tip # 2 ~ Set a Simple Reminder

Attach taking an action to de-stress—like a deep breath—to a simple activity you do several times a day. Whenever

you pick up your keys, get in the car or hang up the phone or feel a stone in your pocket, remember to breathe or do one of the other quick stress tips.

Set your calendar alarm on the computer at the beginning of the day to remind you to take an action to de-stress every hour.

—Why It Works—

We are creatures of habit.

Setting a reminder for a few weeks will begin to condition your body and mind to create the habit of de-stressing.

After a few weeks, you may find yourself naturally doing your de-stress action regularly without the reminder.

Quick Tip # 3 ~ Eat Regularly

Food fuels the cells to provide health and energy. Research indicates that certain foods or lack of them can influence your moods too.

Eat a Green Salad
A green leafy salad not only provides the energy of the sun transformed by the green plants but also provides B-complex vitamins and increases dopamine, which helps to improve mood and reduce stress. Spinach and lettuce contain magnesium, a mineral with relaxing and calming effects, and folic acid, which helps prevent depression.

Throw some tuna or salmon on that salad. According to some studies, consuming more omega-3 acids found in fatty fish like salmon, herring, tuna and sardines may help ease symptoms of depression and hostile or aggressive behavior by raising serotonin levels in the brain.

Then add a few seeds and nuts to your salad. Selenium found in sunflower seeds and Brazil nuts can help anxiety and irritability.

Finally, toss in a few oranges, which are high in vitamin C, to reduce irritability and fatigue. Vitamin C can also help improve serotonin and dopamine levels.

Do you hate salad, raw veggies and whole foods? Then take some high-quality supplements. I recommend several awesome whole food supplements in the Resources section at the end of this book.

—Why It Works—

A small change in eating creates a huge increase in energy levels immediately and in health over time. Your cells need nutrients to produce energy for work and to regenerate when they are under stress.

Fast food, sugar and salt have a deteriorating effect on the body. Sugar provides a temporary high but, to balance that, the body will rebound with an equal or greater low. You actually have less energy in the end.

Eating a little bit of nutritious food every few hours also has side benefits. When your body knows you are going to feed it regularly, it stops packing on fat to prevent you from starving.

Quick Tip # 4 ~ Pack Healthy Munchies

Pack a piece of fruit, some nuts, raisins or other quick snacks to have on hand when you work beyond meal

breaks. Make it something you can grab fast instead of donuts, candy or fast food from the vending machine.

Grab a Zip-Loc bag, throw in a few unsalted nuts, dried berries, raisins, or other dried fruits or natural foods you like and put it in your pocket, purse or desk. Take a handful or two whenever you feel a hunger pang or drop in energy.

—Why It Works—

A little planning to have energizing nibbles you like on hand quickly goes a long way.

It provides a realistic alternative to grabbing caffeine or something that will make you feel worse after you eat it.

This can help you set a new healthier habit that provides quick energy and reduces consumption of empty calories.

When you eat foods that lack adequate nutrition (empty calories), your body is still hungry, so you still want to eat again in a few minutes.

Quick Tip # 5 ~ Drink Water

Most of us have gotten into the habit of drinking things our body cannot use like sugar, caffeine and carbonated drinks.

 Replace one beverage a week with pure water and feel the rejuvenation. Each week replace another cup of coffee or soda with a glass of water.

Over a few weeks, you will find that your body prefers water. Keep a mug of water on your desk or strap on one of those water bottles so you always have some with you. Sip it all day long.

Once your body gets used to the idea that you will be giving it the water it needs regularly, it will stop retaining fluid. Your drinking and peeing ratio will level out in a couple of days.

As your cells rehydrate, you will look and feel younger and more vibrant.

—Why It Works—

Your cells are mostly water. You need to replace the water lost from sweating, tears and the body's heating and cooling system on a continuous basis.

Dehydration is associated with decreased energy, increased hunger, tiredness and aging, wrinkled skin. In addition to drinking water, eat more water-based foods, like fresh fruits and vegetables for hydration.

Another good reason for replacing carbonated beverages with water is that carbonation leaches minerals from your body.

Quick Tip # 6 ~ Rest & Stretch

Take a break when possible. Studies prove that workers who take a break increase productivity.

While you are taking that break, SSSSSStretch!

Have you ever watched animals like a cat or a dog stretch? Most animals stretch regularly. You need regular stretching too.

Take a moment to stand up and stretch. A good stretch decreases stress and increases energy. Energy can become stagnant from sitting too long at your desk or in front of the computer or TV.

If you decided to set a reminder to breathe on stress-buster number two, take a moment to stretch at the same time.

All of your muscles can use stretching from time to time. Stretch your fingers, arms, wrists, ankles, legs, toes, waist, neck and spine.

The small investment in a moment or two of stretching will pay off in reduced stress, clearer thinking and increased productivity.

See the Recommended Resources section of this book for an online stretching site.

—Why It Works—

Stretching improves elasticity and mobility, which allows for relaxed movement and less tension.

Resting the body and mind to a state of quiet opens the senses for more presence in the moment, creativity and peace.

When you create some spaces in your day, you experience more of what is present and come up with creative solutions to stressful situations.

Quick Tip # 7 ~ Give Yourself a Real Break

While you are taking your break at work, home or school, make it a real break for your body by combining quick tips 1–6!

Stretch, have a glass of water, eat some of those nutritional snacks, take a deep breath into the floor of your pelvis, let it out and smile. Feel the return of energy and relaxation to your body, clarity to your mind and caring to your heart.

When you feel stressed, try these simple tips for renewing your body in efficient combinations of breathing, eating, drinking water and rest.

Experience for yourself how taking care of YOU provides the precious resources you need to do what needs to be done from a place of strength and abundance.

—Why It Works—

It is efficient!

You feel even more relaxed and energized in a shorter time by combining two or more of the healthy actions for your body on any break during the day.

Quick Tip # 8 ~ Get It Out

Your body is a container for stress. Holding stress inside your body creates a pressure cooker effect. Like a pressure cooker, the more pressure builds, the more energy you need to keep it contained. This is distressful.

Letting the stress out of your body periodically is vital to releasing the pressure and increasing availability of eustress energy.

You can:
Write it out in a journal. If you are afraid someone will find your notes, burn them. Make it a ritual of getting rid of the stress from the worry or concern you cannot do anything about.

- Talk it out with a confidant, friend or counselor.
- Sweat it out with exercise, a walk, dancing or sports.
- Pound it out on a pillow or stomp your feet.
- Cry it out.
- Scream it out.
- Pray it out.
- Write it out.

—Why It Works—

Releasing the tension releases the energy that is bound up in trying to keep all the stress tightly contained in your body.

Over time, keeping tension held tightly in your body is like being a pressure cooker. Keeping the lid on the pot is exhausting. Moreover, after years of stuffing the stress, just one small event or issue can trigger the lid blowing.

Letting off steam regularly can keep you from blowing your lid.

My Plan for Body De-Stressing

What does renewed health and energy feel like in my body?

_____
_____
_____

How do I look when my body is de-stressed?

_____
_____
_____
_____
_____

What daily action will I commit to this week to achieve these results?

_____
_____
_____
_____

I, _____ will:

_____
_____
_____
_____

My results:

_____
_____
_____
_____

Chapter 5

De-Stressing Your Mind

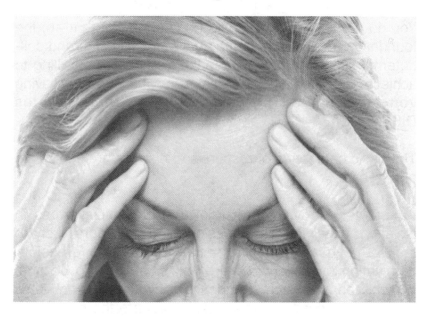

Understanding Control

The mind is a wonderful tool for observation, imagining, processing information and, in short, thinking. However, when the tool becomes the master, stress is inevitable.

Like a computer, your mind holds a massive amount of data. It also has a program to organize those data. Each mind programs the input it receives through unique perceptions and interpretations developed in early childhood. This childhood template is your mind's operating system until you choose to change it.

De-stressing involves becoming aware of and updating these childhood beliefs.

Two core sets of beliefs—who you think you are (self concept) and who you think you "should" be (self ideal)—evolve from what we hear, see and experience as children.

You do not knowingly choose the self images that are the foundation for self-esteem, the value for yourself, and self-determination, the power to make free choices. Failing to achieve this unrealistic self ideal is inevitable, and believing you have limited power to choose freely creates DISTRESS.

The basic categories of response to distress are fight, flight and freeze.

Is your tendency to run, hide and internalize stress in isolation, passivity or depression? Are you more likely to lash out, attack and externalize stress in aggression, domination or anxiety? Or are you most likely to become immobilized and stuck? Regardless of your preferred stress reaction, the core issues and solutions are the same.

The tips that follow are simple, logical and doable. Implementation may be challenging, though. There are additional resources to support you in using these tips at the end of this book.

Quick Tip # 9 ~ Sort Your Stressors

The Serenity Prayer
*God grant me the serenity
to accept the things I cannot change;
courage to change the things I can;
and wisdom to know the difference.*
—Reinhold Niebuhr

The key to mental de-stressing is to recognize the areas of life in which you do or do not have control.

Make a list of ten things, situations or people that stress you.

1._____
2._____
3._____
4._____
5._____
6._____
7._____
8._____
9._____
10._____

Do you see a common theme to your stressors?

If you are like most people, you blame everything outside of you for your stress and direct most of your precious time and energy into fruitless efforts to control the uncontrollable. A short list of uncontrollables includes:
- Time – not enough, what happened in the past, worry about the future
- Nature – illness, aging, death, weather
- Other People – what they think, feel, say or do

The Facts of Life
You have NO control of anything outside yourself.
You have TOTAL control of everything inside yourself.

This does not seem earth-shattering until you look at daily reactions to what stresses you.

You reduce your stress when you put your time and energy into the one area where it will pay off, where you have total control and power to direct your life – in YOU. Put your energy into knowing how you think and feel and making choices about what is important to you. This brings you the confidence and freedom of Self-Mastery.

The Stress Sorter

	I CAN Control	I CANNOT Control
Take Action	**Self-Mastery** (Self-awareness, choice, low stress)	**Endless Striving** (Constant struggle, high stress)
No Action	**Giving Up** (Victim, defeat, high stress)	**Letting Go** (Release, low stress)

Spending time and energy continuously striving to control what is out of your hands is frustrating and useless. The result is high stress. When you find yourself ceaselessly striving to change something outside of yourself with no results, it is time for an inner change.

Giving up your power to make choices for yourself to others results in a hopeless victimized feeling. This is a high-stress area. People frequently seek escape from the high stress of giving up through substances and other addictive behaviors.

On the other hand, letting go of what you cannot control releases you to focus on what is within your power, thus reducing stress. Letting go is accepting the truth that some things, like time, weather and the choices of other people, are simply out of your hands.

Sort your stressors into two areas: those you can and cannot control. Then, spending your time and energy in the areas of Self-Mastery, mastering your understanding of yourself and your choices and Letting Go of what you cannot control will radically reduce your stress!

—Why It Works—

Sorting what you can and cannot control helps you see clearly where to place your attention.

Although the conditioned mind (ego) does not accept change easily, it does like structure.

When you provide a new way to sort thinking that makes logical sense, the mind is more willing to consider it.

Taking charge of what you can control —You— is empowering. This produces eustress for wisdom, creativity and goal achievement.

Letting go of what you cannot control stops useless energy drain that keeps you stuck in endlessly striving to change things that are out of your hands.

Giving up is stressful because you abdicate your power to choose what you can change. You are giving up on yourself and your choices.

Quick Tip # 10 ~ Focus on Choosing Now

Focus your attention on the power to make choices. You can only make choices in the present moment. The past is a memory and the future has not arrived.

You can make informed choices by learning from the past. Today's choices influence the future. Choosing consciously what you do in this moment is the most powerful and least stressful thing you can do.

There is a finite amount of time in a day. You control what you choose to do with it. Prioritizing what is most important to you is essential. Then it is easier to see what must either be delegated or dropped from the "to do" list.

Life becomes much simpler, less stressful and more productive when you are realistic about what you can do and take responsibility for acting on that priority in the present moment. Focus on being aware of your choices today and notice how outcomes change.

Ask yourself frequently, "What is the best use of my time right now?"

The decisions you make moment by moment determine the direction your life takes. Choose your direction wisely today,

—Why It Works—

You are the only person who has control of your choices. Taking charge of your choices reduces stress because it puts you in the driver's seat of your life.

Recognize that choosing not to take action is also your choice.

In consciously choosing, you have the power to influence the direction and satisfaction of your future. You also influence, not control, everyone around you by the choices you make.

Choices made in the past do not need to limit your current choices.

Let go of judgments about the past and learn its lessons. In this way, you can be free to choose differently today.

Quick Tip # 11 ~ Observe Your Mind

What reactions is your mind having to the idea of change? Is it resistant ("This will never work"), distracting ("Let's do something else") or criticizing ("What makes you think you can succeed at being less stressed")? The mind resists changing core beliefs.

Observe its resistance. You do not need to accept or act on what your mind chatters to you all day long. Become a curious observer of the verbal tapes your mind runs.

This running of old tapes (conditioned beliefs) is a function of the conditioned mind. When the tapes are particularly self critical, the name for this function is the "inner critic" or "bully." It is a powerful force against making changes in your life.

In childhood, your mind formed ideas about how to be safe in the world. The conditioned mind (ego) is all about safety and survival. It gets scared when you decide not to play your life by the old "safe" rules. Like a parent, it is still telling you what to do and judging your performance, often harshly.

Although the survival functions of the brain are important, you are no longer a vulnerable infant or child. The primitive fight, flight and freeze responses are limited strategies for managing adult life and relationships.

Observe your mental directives. What are the words your mind uses to keep you tied to old rules? What is the tone of voice? Whose voice does it sound like? Mom? Dad? Someone else?

Keep a journal of your observations. Looking over your journal can give you clues to the patterns or specific "rules" that still inform your choices today. One of mine was, "If you say what you really think, people won't like you." Then my mind would ruminate over things I said, constantly judging the potential impact. This rule was time-wasting, relationship-stifling and professionally defeating, all with the good intention to keep me "safe" from criticism.

When you take the position of observing your mind with curiosity, instead of believing and allowing it to bully you by what it says, you can free yourself from the mental stress these messages cause.

—*Why It Works*—

You are not your thoughts.

The purpose of your mind is to support your decision-making, not control it.

While the original unconscious program was useful in keeping you safe as a child, you must consciously update that program so it can serve you in being a powerful, response-able adult.

Observing how your mind works helps you to realize you are free to change your thinking and puts you back in control of your life.

When you have control, you feel less stressed.

Quick Tip # 12 ~ Stop "Shoulding" on Yourself

Take decisive action to stop the inner critic.

Whenever you hear your inner voice spouting its "shoulds,"

"shouldn'ts" or judgments (negative or positive), take action to stop the thought.

Each inner voice is unique. If yours is aggressive or hostile, you will want to stop it with some force. You can think or say aloud, "Stop!" or use more colorful language. My inner critic is manipulative, with a tone of helpfulness. My approach is, "Thank you for sharing," then promptly let it go.

Drop the image of who you think you "should" be. This is a composite made up by various people, none of whom lives your unique life. I call it the *Perfection Myth*, an ideal image that does not exist in reality. You spend most of your precious time and energy trying to achieve that image or feeling like a failure because you can't.

A helpful strategy when you hear the words "should" or "should not" in your mind is to ask the question, "Who made that up?" Realize that there are only a few laws of nature. Human beings made up everything else.

Some beliefs are useful for living comfortably in society. Choose the ones you want to keep and let the rest go.

Replace the old rules with supportive ones. From my earlier example (Tip # 11), "If you say what you really think, people won't like you," I counter with, "By speaking my truth, others can connect with me and connect with their truth."

The mind runs the programming you feed it. Feed it with care. Choose to surround yourself with the books, TV, movies, magazines, people and experiences that support and sustain your life and uplift your outlook.

Here is an example of the things people make up that are not necessarily useful or true.

The Erroneous Concept of Work-Life Balance

For most of us, especially women, work and life are not separate entities.

All the categories we separate life into are artificial, including weekdays and weekends. Life flows continuously from birth to death.

If you look at a balance scale, you will see that the two pans on each side are not separate; they connect at the center fulcrum.

Imagine that one pan holds your lifetime, the other your life experience. This is your time-life balance. The fulcrum is YOU.

The time side is finite. You have no idea how much you have. The great news is that you get to choose what to place on the experience side of the scale.

To reduce your stress: Choose wisely every moment of every day and be engaged fully in whatever you choose!

—Why It Works—

Conditioning and images are not the truth about who you are or "should" be. They are unconscious programs running your precious life as if you were still a child.

The mind, like a computer, uses an operating system. Your life is continuously changing. How will your computer serve you if you never update the operating system to keep up with changing technology or delete out-of-date files to clear the space for new information?

Your mind requires continuous monitoring and updating in order to serve you in consciously choosing the life you want in this moment.

Quick Tip # 13 ~ Turn Off the News

This is a huge time-saver as well as a stress-saver.

Today's news is less about objective reporting and more about improving ratings through entertainment.

The goal is to grab and keep your attention by using language and emotions that tend to sensationalize and stimulate interest with fear, horror and other heightened stressful emotions.

I am not suggesting you ignore the news but rather not dwell on it for more than a few minutes to get the headlines and the basic information you need.

Especially do not start or end your day with negative news.

It is important to start your day with something uplifting or inspirational. Choose something that gives you a positive feeling and focus for the day.

Turn off the news at least 30 minutes before retiring for the night. At the very least, do not leave it on for your unconscious mind to absorb while you sleep.

If you need sound to fall asleep, try a soothing sound machine or relaxation CD. See Recommended Resources at the end of this book.

—Why It Works—

What you feed your mind is just as important as what you feed your body.

Your brain is like a computer. What you input on a daily basis becomes its truth. In computer-ese, the saying is GIGO – "Garbage In, Garbage Out."

If you feed your mind heavy meals of negativity, violence and situations over which you have no control, your mind dwells on fear and powerlessness.

What your mind focuses on expands and becomes your reality.

You choose the reality you want to live by focusing your mind on what you want to increase in your life.

Just as inspiration of fresh air de-stresses your body, inspiring information is healthy for your mind.

Quick Tip # 14 ~ Don't Worry, Be Happy

The result of your mind's persistent and fruitless efforts to predict and control the future is "worry."

Worry is a learned mental habit. Daily conversations and media speculations about possible disasters reinforce worry.

Your mental stress increases to the extent that you engage in worrisome conversations and feed your mind negative speculation about a future you cannot control.

Energy tied up in worry is not available to make wise productive choices in this moment. You have the power to influence the future through choices you make today.

You can harness and use your mind's fascination with the future by envisioning the future you want, rather than the future you fear.

Fill your mind with images of a desired future and use your mind to plan the steps to achieve that future. This gives you a blueprint upon which you can make purposeful and enjoyable choices today that can influence desired outcomes tomorrow.

A vision board is a tool you can use for feeding your mind images of a desired future. You can find resources for a vision board in Chapter 10.

Envisioning a positive future does not predict or control its outcome. You can influence the direction of your future by choosing the images you feed your mind today.

Choose what you want, rather than worrying about what you don't want. This increases your happiness and reduces your stress.

—Why It Works—

Because the future is unknown, unpredictable and uncontrollable, spending time and energy worrying about the future is a huge source of stress.

You feel powerless and victimized when you focus on what you cannot control.

Your present choices are always within your control.

The future, like all of life, is full of possibilities. You have the power to choose the direction you want by imagining the future you desire. In this way you exercise the greatest influence you can on your future.

My Plan for Mind De-Stressing

How do I see myself thinking and acting with a clear and calm mind?

_____
_____
_____

How do I see myself making conscious choices and relating with others?

_____
_____
_____
_____
_____

What daily action will I commit to this week to achieve these results?

_____
_____
_____
_____

I, _____ will:

_____
_____
_____

My results:

_____
_____
_____
_____
_____

Chapter 6

De-Stressing Your Emotions

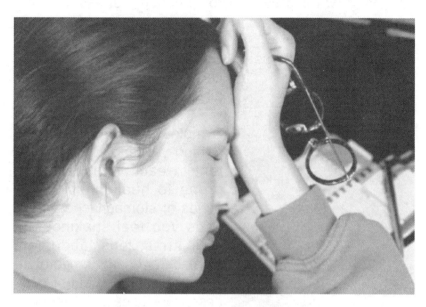

Fear: Facts and Fallacies

Emotional stress comes from your reaction to fear. Anytime you feel threatened by situations you cannot control, fear arises. Emotions express fear with responses such as anxiety, frustration, anger, hatred, powerlessness, sadness, grief, depression and more.

How do your emotions signal you that a situation or person is presenting a threat to your survival? Once you know your emotional stress signs, you can take actions to free yourself of perceived threats.

Emotional stress drains your energy and wears out the body. Being aware of your early physical signs of emotional stress, understanding your underlying fear, taking control of yourself and tapping on your energy meridians are all effective ways to reduce emotional stress.

Quick Tip # 15 ~ Pay Attention to Signals

The early warning system for emotional stress is in the body.

Observing the patterns of stress symptoms in your body

can help you detect emotionally stressful situations quickly.

Symptoms vary from person to person yet tend to be consistent in each of us. Are you prone to headaches, backaches or stomachaches? Perhaps you feel shakiness in your arms, legs, abdomen, stomach or heart. Temperature changes such as heat or coolness, sweaty palms or feet can also be signals that something is not quite right in a situation.

Once you identify your unique body reactions to stress, you can take action to address the early emotional stress symptoms before the reaction becomes unbearable or debilitating or before you say or do something you may regret.

Emotions are neither good nor bad; they are an early warning system that alerts you to danger. De-stressing your emotions requires awareness. Pay attention to your emotional symptoms rather than ignoring, judging, wishing them away or medicating them. This is the first step in understanding and taking action to reduce emotional stress.

Your body, based on past experiences, picks up subtle signs in a situation that alert you to danger. When some element in a situation reminds the body of a danger experienced in the past, it sends an immediate message to the nervous system. The stress response makes the body ready for battle or ready to run. This is your unique "fight, flight or freeze" response. The response activates your nervous system, making you physically ready to handle the dangerous situation.

The body readies a physical response, even when the danger is about an emotional fear. Fear of disappointment, lack of recognition, making a mistake or other emotionally charged feelings can summon the physical fear response.

The sooner you recognize your fear response, the sooner you can address it and return your body to a relaxed state.

Being on "red alert" for long periods of time wears out the body. Some examples of long-term emotional wear and tear include ulcers, headaches, backaches, heart disease, irritable bowel syndrome, chronic fatigue and fibromyalgia.

—Why It Works—

We are beings of habit. Past conditioning inhibits freedom of choice. Awareness of patterns is the first step in freeing yourself from this conditioning.

When you understand the perceived threat, you can take rational steps to correct the situation or your perception of it.

Ignoring emotional signals will not make the threat go away. Your emotional response will continue to escalate until you pay attention, even if that means putting you into bed with a debilitating illness.

☀ Quick Tip # 16 ~ Address the Underlying Fear

Ask the questions, "What am I afraid of?" or "In what way do I feel something in this situation is out of my control?" Then address the real fear or control issue.

For example, if you have a fear of making a mistake in a situation, you can ask for help, refresh your skill in that area by reading or practicing or reassure yourself by remembering all the times you accomplished tasks successfully.

Sometimes the underlying fear is not obvious. Assess the elements in the situation. Are some or all of these elements present at other times when you feel stressed? Is there a particular type of personality or situation that consistently stresses you? Look for patterns. These can be clues to reveal underlying fears.

Often the original stressor is a memory from childhood that the body is still signaling as a fearsome situation even though, as an adult, you are completely capable of handling it. In these situations, the stress response may not seem logical, yet your body is giving you stress signals.

Tip # 21, the Emotional Freedom Technique (EFT), is a useful tool for clearing these memories and patterns.

—Why It Works—

Most of our modern emotional reactions are based in old childhood experiences when we were vulnerable and powerless to make free choices.

When you assess the real threat to your survival in this moment, you create the opportunity to update those perceptions and reactions.

This enhances self-mastery (see Tip # 9), which empowers you to choose new responses.

Quick Tip # 17 ~ Reestablish Inner Control

When your energy and attention is scattered in too many directions and you feel frantic, take a moment to take a  deep breath, feel your feet on the ground and reestablish your inner control and balance.

Taking control of your own energy and ground are the first steps to realizing you do have control over your reactions and your choices in the situation.

You may not have control over changes or additional responsibilities in your work assignment or the scheduling of your kids' ball games, yet you can control your choice of how to act, think or feel in the midst of pressures and changes.

Every apparent crisis also has within it the opportunity to learn or try something new.

When you are in control of your inner calm, you can think more clearly, become aware of expanded options and make better choices.

—Why It Works—

Within any situation there are elements within your control like breathing, thinking, feeling and personal action.

When you start focusing on controlling your inner response, the things outside your control become more emotionally manageable.

Quick Tip # 18 ~ Smile

Smiling not only reduces your stress but reduces the stress of the people around you. Smiling is contagious.

In this nurse's opinion, attitude is more contagious than the common cold.

It's hard to smile and also be thinking about something negative or depressing. The smile itself can change your mood instantly.

What makes you smile? Is there a picture, a gift or some experience or memory that makes you smile every time you see it or think about it?

Place a copy of that photo or a memento or symbol of the experience that makes you smile in places where you will see them many times in the day.

If you do not have an office or a stationary place where you spend most of your time, put a charm on your key chain to remind you of that thing that makes you smile.

Here is an empowering thought:

Realize that the first race of your life was the one that resulted in the fertilization of the egg that became YOU. You already won the human race!

Are you smiling?

—Why It Works—

Studies show that smiling improves your immune system and increases endorphins and serotonin, which reduces stress. Smiling can also reduce high blood pressure.

Quick Tip # 19 ~ Feel the Support

Often stress comes from the perception that you are alone and unsupported. Changing that perception can change your stress in an instant.

Start by feeling the ground under your feet. Feel the support of the earth beneath you. Feel the support of the chair you're sitting in, the seat under your bottom and the back meeting your back. Take a breath and realize the support of the atmosphere in providing the oxygen you need to stay alive.

Support is all around you. You just don't think about it this way.

Do you have a sense of spiritual support, a power greater than yourself that supports your existence? You may call that power the Source, Life Force, God, Allah, Great Spirit, Consciousness or some other name (see Quick Tip # 30).

Are you the kind of person who tries to do it all yourself? When you feel like you alone are carrying the world on your shoulders, those shoulders can begin to sag or tighten up with stiffness and pain. It's time to let go of over-responsibility.

"Let Go and Let God" is a motto in 12-step recovery programs. A friend of mine once quipped, "Life got a lot better once I resigned as CEO of the universe."

Who are the people supporting you in some way—family, friends, community services or your employer? If you are not feeling the support, examine how willing you are to receive support.

Being a gracious receiver is as admirable as being an effective giver. Find an opportunity today to receive support from another person with graciousness and appreciation.

—Why It Works—

Human beings are social beings. We have basic needs for relationship, interaction, touch and support.

Being open to support has a leveling effect on relationships, which strengthens the bond between people.

Feeling supported reduces the stressful feelings of loneliness and vulnerability.

Quick Tip # 20 ~ Get a Hug, Give a Hug

Stretch your arms out in front of you, wrap them around your body and give yourself a big hug. Feel the warmth of your arms across your heart and feel the caress of your hands. You deserve to feel appreciated.

I've read that you need four hugs a day for survival, eight for maintenance and twelve for growth. I don't know if that's true, but I do know that a hug at the right time can do wonders for reducing your stress.

Sharing hugs with others is also great. Two or more people can benefit from the same hug. It's a good idea to make sure the other person is willing to have a hug.

A HUG

No moving parts, no batteries.
No monthly payments and no fees;
Inflation proof, non-taxable,
In fact, it's quite relaxable.
It can't be stolen, won't pollute,
One size fits all, do not dilute.
It uses little energy,
But yields results enormously,
Relieves your tension and your stress,
Invigorates your happiness;
Combats depression, makes you beam,
And elevates your self esteem!
Your circulation it corrects
Without unpleasant side effects.
It is, I think, the perfect drug:
May I prescribe, my friend...the hug!
(and, of course, fully returnable!)
—author unknown

—Why It Works—

This action satisfies the human need for touch and connection.

Quick Tip # 21 ~ Tap on It

Tapping on acupressure points is an efficient and effective way to deal with emotional stress.

 The Emotional Freedom Technique (EFT) is simple, powerful and the best technique I have found for immediate stress reduction. It works for children as well as adults for a variety of issues.

There are four parts to this technique: identify the symptom or stressor and its intensity, set up the issue, tap on the acupressure points and integrate the resolution. You can access a video demonstration of these steps at www.ailaspeaks.com/eft.html.

Step 1: Identify the specific stressor, such as tension in the right shoulder, shakiness in the abdomen, fear of making a mistake doing ____, anger at Mr. __ for saying ____. Assign a number on a scale of 0 (low) to 10 (high), indicating the intensity level you feel.

Step 2: Set up the issue. While tapping on the edge of your palm (on either hand, the spot where you would chop a karate board), say (aloud, if possible), "Even though I have this (name the specific issue), I deeply and completely accept myself." Tap and repeat the phrase three times.

Step 3: Tap on the points—the top of the head (baby soft spot area), eyebrow, side of the eye, under the eye (all eye points are on the orbital bone), under the nose, in the chin groove, on the collarbone, on the side of the body (about two inches below the armpit). Often the stress reduces or disappears by just tapping the face and body points. If not, go on to tap the finger points on the side of the finger about where the nail and skin meet—the thumb, first finger, middle finger, baby finger. Use either hand, either side of the body. Reassess your intensity level.

Step 4: Integrate the resolution. Using four fingers, tap in the groove on the back of your hand between the knuckles of the ring finger and baby finger (the Gamut Point) while you do these movements: close your eyes, open your eyes. Without moving your head, look down hard to the left and right, roll your eyes clockwise and counterclockwise, hum briefly, count to five and hum briefly again. Reassess your intensity level.

You can do these steps several times until the physical stress reaction subsides. You may want to learn more about this technique or consult a practitioner to use it most effectively.

You can find additional EFT information and tools in the Recommended Resources section at the end of this book.

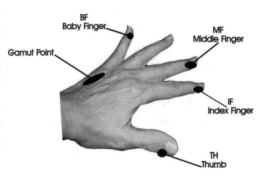

BF
Baby Finger

MF
Middle Finger

Gamut Point

IF
Index Finger

TH
Thumb

—Why It Works—

We are energy beings. Energy moves through the energetic meridians of the body. This is the basis for acupuncture and other energy techniques.

When energy is stuck, you have a physical or emotional response. Tapping on the junctures of these meridians loosens the stuck energy so you feel more relaxed.

Quick Tip # 22 ~ Be Grateful

Gratitude on the simplest level allows you to appreciate the very basic moments of your life. It allows you to live fully in this moment and stimulates your heart to smile.

> *"Let us rise up and be thankful, for if we didn't learn a lot today, at least we learned a little, and if we didn't learn a little, at least we didn't get sick, and if we got sick, at least we didn't die; so, let us all be thankful."*
>
> **—Buddha—**

Once the mind and heart turn their attention toward gratitude, life improves instantly.

So much of the mind's focus is set on what is not yet, if only... and what if? How much time does your mind spend on regrets from the past or projections or desires for the future?

When you accomplish a goal, do you take time to celebrate or "goal vault" right on to the next items on your "to do" list?

Taking a moment to notice one small thing (water, a place to live) for which you are grateful stops the stressed mind in its tracks. The mind makes a U-turn and begins to find more opportunities to be grateful. Delight grows and expands.

A fringe benefit of the energy of gratitude is that it attracts more opportunities to be grateful. This is the Law of Attraction or the Law of Resonance. What you focus on expands!

Take a moment to be grateful right now.

Start a gratitude journal. Get a small note pad and pen to put beside your bed at night. Write five things you are grateful for each day before you fall asleep.

The unconscious mind believes what you feed it. Feed it gratitude before sleep and watch your life change.

—Why It Works—

Momentum: A body in motion tends to continue to move in the same direction. This is also true for gratitude. Gratitude inspires more awareness of the things for which you are grateful.

This is not only satisfying in the moment but energetically attracts more desired outcomes into your life.

My Plan for Emotional De-Stressing

How do I look and feel when I am calm and confident?

_____

_____

_____

How do I see myself responding rather than reacting to situations?

_____

_____

_____

_____

_____

What daily action will I commit to this week to achieve these results?

_____

_____

_____

_____

I, _____ will:

_____

_____

_____

My results:

_____

_____

_____

_____

Chapter 7

De-Stressing Your Spirit

Connecting with Life

Loss of zest, life purpose or perceived identity stresses the human spirit. Spiritual stress results from the loss of connection to your true self, values, purpose, nature and vibrations.

How you define who you are and the meaning and purpose of life is core to the health of your spirit. You experience spiritual stress when these definitions are challenged or unclear. The human spirit asks, "Who am I?", "What is life about?" and "What is my purpose?"

These questions peak at times of significant life change or loss, as in the identity challenges of adolescence and mid-life or the loss of a child, spouse, job or body part.

Attaching identity and purpose to variables outside your control makes you vulnerable to spiritual stress.

An example: When I was supporting nurses in addiction recovery who had lost their licenses to practice their work as nurses, one of the first challenges was to realize that losing their identity as nurses did not mean they lost their identity as human beings. "If who I am is a nurse, then losing my job means losing my self."

You are the same being you were at birth. Your body changes year by year, your thinking changes with new knowledge and experience, your emotions change moment to moment, but none of these defines WHO you ARE.

Your body, thoughts, feelings and experiences are the expressions of your life, not the definitions of your being.

Taking time every day to clarify and reconnect with yourself and your nature reduces spiritual stress and supports happiness, security and inner peace.

Quick Tip # 23 ~ Connect with Your Self

Look deep into your eyes in a mirror.

Who is looking back?

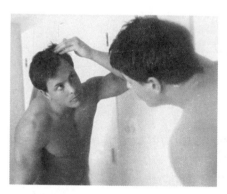

Realize that the same awareness inside of you today has been there from the beginning of your life.

Your body, emotions and thoughts change, yet abiding through the changes is an unchanging You.

This invulnerable core is a foundation for inner strength and support.

You are able to observe your experiences of and responses to life. Human beings have the capacity to observe, reflect and be conscious about our lives.

To the extent that you can strengthen and support the curiosity of your inner observer, you will reduce your stress.

—Why It Works—

When you are not dependent on outer conditions to define yourself, you feel free.

The outer world is constantly changing and undependable. Your inner being is solid, grounded in reality and invulnerable to attack by others.

Viktor Frankl powerfully describes this concept in _Man's Search for Meaning_. His experiences in a concentration camp stripped him of all external connections to the experience of being human. All he had left was his inner consciousness. He concluded this was the ultimate source of his strength of being.

Quick Tip # 24 ~ Connect with the Moment

Feel the water on your hands as you wash them. Notice the specific way you wash them, the slipperiness of the soap, the temperature of the water. Feel your feet on the

ground, notice the sights, sounds and smells around you.

Sensing your experience in this moment is a practice in being present that helps you connect with life in a deep and meaningful way.

Set an intention at the beginning of your day to stop and be present frequently. You will find this practice reduces stress by increasing awareness, connection and meaning in each moment.

This approach to experiencing life is "mindfulness."

—*Why It Works*—

Connecting to the present moment centers, relaxes and enlivens your life experience.

You are not ruminating about the past or worrying about the future, which are stressful because they are out of your control.

This moment is your lifetime, the only moment in which you can live. Once it is gone, the next moment arrives to be experienced.

The moment-by-moment Gift of Life is the Present.

When you are aware of the insight, knowledge and experience this moment offers, you have a sense of control within your self, which reduces stress.

![sun icon] Quick Tip # 25 ~ Connect with Your Purpose

How do you know what is important to you?

You feel it. Notice the small voice or sense of knowing inside when something is attracting you. Your body alerts

you to what elements in your life are dangerous or attractive long before your mind can explain why.

Pay attention to those cues. This is your intuition, or sixth sense. Your deepest values and purpose are not in your head but in your heart. To what does your heart respond? What touches your spirit? What energizes you or inspires you?

Purpose is a force that energizes. It inspires you to get up in the morning. What excites your passion for life?

Check out the resources in Chapter 10 for finding your gifts, purpose and passion.

—Why It Works—

When your inner promptings guide you, you cannot make a mistake. These are signs that lead to your truest desires and lasting happiness.

Joseph Campbell, the great mythologist, advised, "Follow your bliss."

When you follow your true path or calling, you are invigorated, rather than stressed.

Quick Tip # 26 ~ Connect with Nature

You are part of a larger cosmos. You are not isolated, as the boundaries of your body suggest.

Mud Puddle Reflection by A. Accad

"Nature is doing her best each moment to make us well."
—Henry David Thoreau—

Whether you look at life from a religious, spiritual or scientific perspective, what you think and feel affects the environment and the environment affects you. Spending time in nature reconnects you to your natural rhythms.

It is easy to lose your center when attending to other people, television, the computer, shopping and so on constantly captures your attention.

Taking time every day to be quiet in a natural setting, reflecting, journaling or just being present can bring you back to yourself.

Take a moment to smell a flower, watch the river flow by or appreciate a tree when you take a break or before going home at the end of the workday.

—Why It Works—

Earth vibrates at a certain frequency.

Spending time in nature synchronizes our vibrations to the natural vibrations that support us.

Closed up all day in hermetically sealed buildings with fluorescent lighting and recirculating air can cause a loss of balance and connection with your self and your natural rhythms.

◉ Quick Tip # 27 ~ Connect with Nature Indoors

If you cannot go out, at least look out a window. If there isn't a window available, put a part of nature in your space, like flowers, water, seashells, rocks or even a photo of nature.

When you are out of touch with the natural world, it is easy to lose perspective. You can get out of touch with your self and your connection to the larger world.

Reconnecting with the vibration of nature is a way to come home to the reality of your existence in a tangible way. It helps you feel more alive and centered. This not only reduces stress but increases energy and vitality.

Select natural items from the air (like feathers), earth (like rocks, plants and flowers) or sea (like shells, sand or an aquarium with fish or fountain) or images of these things to include in your work and home environment. Add the elements that appeal most to you or have the calming or energizing effect you prefer.

—*Why It Works*—

Natural plants, rocks, shells all have soothing vibrations that can help you stay connected to your natural rhythms and being.

Even if the items are only images of nature that remind you of an experience, they create the same physiological responses in the body as the experience itself.

An example: When you recall an image of seeing, smelling and tasting lemon, saliva begins to develop in your mouth.

Quick Tip # 28 ~ Connect with Your Vibes

Stress is an energy vibration. You can reduce your stress by using other vibrations that are either soothing or enjoyable to you.

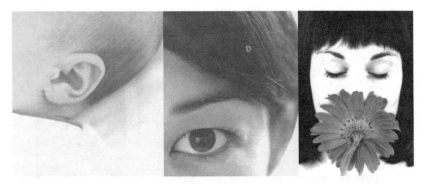

Color, sound, odors, images all have vibrations. Which vibrations resonate with you in a way that soothes, energizes or affects your mood?

Fill the space around you with these vibrations. Paint the walls with color that supports your energy; add images, sounds, textures and fragrances you love. Then observe how you feel in the space you have created.

—Why It Works—

Color, sound, odor, thoughts... everything emits vibrations of energy. Energetic vibrations entrain one another.

When you are around vibrations that are incompatible with you, you do not feel as connected to your nature.

Choosing to surround yourself with vibrations that support your spirit enhances your sense of well-being.

Quick Tip # 29 ~ Listen to the Music

Putting on music that speaks to your soul will instantly change your mood and change your stress.

Music can soothe your jangled nerves and return you to a state of calm, peace or happiness.

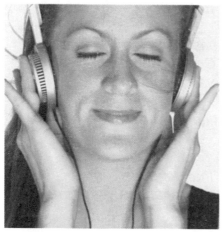

Pay attention to how you feel when you are listening to certain kinds of music. Then select the music that suits you best for reducing your stress. You may want something calming or you might want something enlivening, depending upon your mood or the situation.

Listen to music that makes you smile, feel harmonious or centered.

What kinds of sounds do you listen to all day long? Are you exposed to noise pollution? Do you hear the sounds of motors whirring, phones ringing, people arguing or other sounds that irritate your senses?

When you are around the same sounds all the time, you tend to tune them out of awareness. Even though these sounds are outside of your awareness, their vibrations still affect you.

Whether at work or at home, surrounding yourself with the right vibrations can make a huge difference in your stress.

Introduce some music into your environment and see what happens to your stress level.

—Why It Works—

Music has vibrational energy patterns that affect your energy levels. Certain music may also remind you of happy or sad times.

Listening to music influences the environment and mood.

Select the right music that supports your goal of calmness or motivation or changes your stress level.

☼ Quick Tip # 30 ~ Connect with a Higher Power

Letting go of what you cannot control reduces stress.

When you believe that all life connects in ways beyond your understanding and that there is a Higher Power into which you can entrust those things you cannot control, this reduces stress.

Connection with a Higher Power allows the mind to let go of the belief that everything "should" be within your control.

This tip adds another dimension of support to "Letting Go" of things you cannot control in Tip # 9 ~ Sort Your Stressors.

—Why It Works—

Research by Larry Dossey (Prayer is Good Medicine, 1996) and others has demonstrated that prayer has an effect on healing and health.

Addictive behaviors are a way to handle and escape from stress. Belief in a Higher Power is central to 12-step recovery programs for addictions of all kinds.

My Plan for Spirit De-Stressing

How do I look and act when I am feeling good about me and about my unique contribution to the world?

_____

_____

_____

What am I doing differently when I am focused and taking purposeful action?

_____

_____

_____

_____

_____

What daily action will I commit to this week to achieve these results?

_____

_____

_____

_____

I, _____ will:

_____

_____

_____

My results:

_____

_____

_____

_____

_____

Chapter 8

De-Stressing Your Relationships

Accepting Uniqueness and Equality

The most difficult stressor for most of us is other people.

We often blame other people for our feelings, thoughts and the choices we feel forced to make. The truth is other people are not responsible for any of these things.

When you give others control over your feelings, thoughts and choices, you feel powerlessly stressed.

The natural response to loss of control or the fear of loss is fight, flight or freeze. It's no surprise that as more people feel out of control in their lives, incidents of rage (fight), depression (flight) and chronic illness (freeze) are increasing.

Each human being is unique. This fact is borne out in our DNA, voice patterns and fingerprints.

We express that uniqueness in how we interpret our experience of the world from birth to death. Your beliefs, values, knowledge and experiences are all unique, unmatched by any other person.

When you understand that others have the equal right to think, feel and act according to their own judgment and that they have unique perspectives, you realize that trying to control another person is futile.

In de-stressing a relationship, you are concerned about not only your stress but also the stress of the other person. You want to reduce the fear of loss of control on both sides of the relationship.

Standing in your power to control your side of the relationship is your right and responsibility. At the same time, creating an environment where others know you are respecting their equal rights and responsibility for their unique side of the communication has the potential to reduce their stress as well.

While you do not have the power to control another, you do have the power to influence and persuade others with an attitude of confidence and openness. The power to de-stress your relationships is in your hands.

Agreement is not the basis for stress-free relationships. The basis for healthy relationships is respect, freedom and value of each unique person for the other's equal freedom and right to think, feel, make personal choices and take responsibility for them.

Quick Tip # 31 ~ Take Responsibility for You

When you find yourself reacting to what someone says or does, take a moment to take a deep breath and reflect on where the reaction is coming from. In what way are you feeling a loss of control?

The other person's behavior may remind you of a parent. In this case, you can feel like a powerless child. Remind yourself that you are an adult. You have the right to think, feel and choose according to your beliefs and desires. If there are consequences for your choice, recognize those, assess your options and choose accordingly.

On the other hand, the person's stance may be more like an irresponsible child who is expecting you to take responsibility for his or her feelings and behavior. Clarifying both of your positions as equal adults and separating the responsibility appropriately can reduce your stress.

Caution: If the other person is not willing to take responsibility for his or her behavior, this approach can actually increase his or her stress. Assess your options and choose your response wisely.

Keep in mind, de-stressing is not dependent on what you choose to do. De-stressing is in understanding that your choice is in your control.

—Why It Works—

Adults have the right and responsibility to make their own choices.

When others attempt to control you or you try to control others, stress results.

Stress is reduced when you empower yourself to take responsibility for your thoughts, feelings and choices. Recognizing others' responsibility for their choices also reduces your stress.

Quick Tip # 32 ~ Position for Equality

Reduce your stress by taking charge of your physical, nonverbal power in the relationship.

Make sure you are at a physical position level with the

other person. If he or she is standing, either invite him or her to sit or you stand up.

Stand up straight, feet about shoulder-width apart, and breathe deeply into the base of your pelvis. Maintain direct, open, non-glaring eye contact.

When you want to have a collaborative conversation, sit at an angle beside the other person. If possible, eliminate any barriers like desks between you.

If you anticipate a conversation will be stressful, pick a location that will reduce the stress, such as taking a walk in nature, a neutral or living room-like setting or a space that is open, comfortable and light.

By leveling your position with the other person, you send the message of respect for your equality to the other person. This communicates a desire to be equitable in the communication.

—Why It Works—

Leveling the position with another person in a communication sends a non-verbal message of respect for the equality of both people in the interaction.

Respecting equality and uniqueness in communication reduces the stress caused by the perceived control of one person by the other.

Quick Tip # 33 ~ Let Go of Who Is Right

Every person is unique and has unique experiences that shape his or her understanding.

Just because we may speak the same language, English

for example, does not guarantee that we understand words and expressions in the same way. In fact, none of us understands anything in exactly the same way.

When a relationship or communication exchange is going smoothly, it may be because our meanings and understandings are close enough.

When those meanings are far apart, conflict can occur. Not only do the words or expressions of them not mean the same thing, they can be opposite.

Who is right? Who is wrong? Arguing this point will not resolve the misunderstanding.

You must realize that you have no control over the other person's interpretation or choice to continue to be angry, insulted or disengaged. You only have control of your intention, message and reactions.

Take charge of your end of the exchange and let go of trying to be right in the other person's mind.

Try to see others' perspectives if you can. Realize that they are right from their viewpoint.

There are no winners or losers in a relationship, only people who choose to learn through sharing their different views.

—Why It Works—

Everyone sees things from a unique perspective.

Each person's perspective is correct from his or her vantage point, background and experience.

Attempting to convince someone that his or her perspective is wrong is an effort to control him or her. Controlling what you cannot control creates stress in both people and the relationship between them.

Relationships are not win/lose contests. You do not want your partner in a relationship to feel like a loser.

Imagine a tug–of–war — when one person puts down the rope, the stress on the rope ends and the win-lose contest is over.

Quick Tip # 34 ~ Request Feedback

It is important to realize that everyone has a different perspective and interpretation of what he or she sees and hears. Even though you may both speak the same language, two people will not hear things the same way.

 Making the assumption that people see things the way you do or that they "should" creates stress.

It's important to understand that there are as many ways to view a situation or experience as there are people involved. Requesting feedback with curiosity and an open attitude is an important way to increase clarity and reduce the stress of misunderstanding.

Be sure to take responsibility for your message when requesting feedback. An example would be, "Joe, I just want to be sure I haven't left anything out. Would you be willing to share what you heard me say about _____?"

Your tone is important in requesting feedback. A tone of sincere desire to know what the other person thinks and feels is critical to success. Be curious rather than ready to judge the answer. Remember, the other person has the freedom and right to think, feel and choose his or her responses.

Feedback helps you to learn how the other person sees the situation differently. Respecting his or her willingness to provide feedback gives you the best opportunity to correct misunderstandings and improve relationships.

—Why It Works—

Everyone has a unique perspective.

You have no way to know what is going on in other people's minds unless you ask them and they express their thoughts honestly.

In order to facilitate understanding, you must create an atmosphere where the other person can express what he or she is thinking safely without feeling judged for what he or she says.

Being genuinely curious to know others' perspectives will help them to feel comfortable sharing their viewpoints. This helps you understand them better and communicate more effectively in the future.

My Plan for Relationship De-Stressing

How do I look and act when I am communicating with other people?

_____
_____
_____

What am I doing differently when I am respecting the uniqueness and equality of myself and the other person?

_____
_____
_____
_____

What daily action will I commit to this week to achieve these results?

_____
_____
_____
_____

I, _____ will:

_____
_____
_____

My results:

_____
_____
_____
_____
_____

Chapter 9

My Daily De-Stress Action Plan

(You may want to print or copy these pages to use over again)

Before starting your action plan, describe the nature of your stress now.

My physical stress symptoms include:

_____

_____

My mental stress symptoms include:

_____

_____

My emotional stress symptoms include:

_____

_____

My spiritual stress symptoms include:

_____

_____

My relationship stress symptoms include:

_____

_____

Possible benefits from implementing my de-stress action plan include:

_____

_____

_____

I am ready to commit to taking the actions that will reduce my stress & improve my life!

_____   _____

Name   **Date**

Plan for Week # 1

Select the tip(s) you plan to use this week and when.

Be realistic – One change is a great start!
It is better to start small and achieve success!

Be Persistent – Keep visualizing success!
You may need to try a few tips to find the ones that are perfectly suited to your success.

Before arising
_____
_____

Preparing for the day
_____
_____

At breaks
_____
_____
_____

At mealtimes
_____
_____

After dinner
_____
_____
_____

Before bed
_____
_____

Results

What worked?

_____

_____

_____

What did not work?

_____

_____

_____

Adjusted Plan for Week # 2

Tip(s) I will continue to use

_____

_____

A new tip I will incorporate

_____

_____

How and when I see myself using this tip

_____

_____

How I see myself experiencing the benefits of using this tip
(How I look, feel, act)

_____

_____

_____

_____

Results

What worked?

_____

_____

_____

What did not work?

_____

_____

_____

Adjusted Plan for Week # 3

Tips I will continue to use

_____

_____

_____

A new tip I will incorporate

_____

_____

How and when I see myself using this tip

_____

_____

How I see myself experiencing the benefits of using this tip
(How I look, feel, act)

_____

_____

_____

**Continue to play with your plan
until you find what works for you!**

Adjusted Plan for Week # 4

Reassess your current stress symptoms and results.

My physical stress symptoms include:

_____

_____

My mental stress symptoms include:

_____

_____

My emotional stress symptoms include:

_____

_____

My spiritual stress symptoms include:

_____

_____

The current benefits of implementing my de-stress action plan include:

_____

_____

_____

I am ready to recommit to taking the actions that will reduce my stress & improve my life!

_____   _____

Name   **Date**

Daily Declarations

Declaring truths aloud helps your unconscious mind make adjustments in the old disempowering beliefs that stress you.

Your unconscious mind believes what you tell it. Become more aware of your language, especially the inner critic (tip #12, Stop "Shoulding" On Yourself). When you stop the negative messages, it is helpful to replace them with powerful, truthful messages or declarations.

Over time, these true statements become part of your belief system that supports low stress, empowerment and self-esteem.

On the following pages you'll find some suggested declarations to support your change in thinking.

- Make copies of these statements or just the ones that speak most powerfully to you.

- Put them in places where you will see them each day.

- Say them aloud with conviction.

- Watch your confidence grow!

Daily Declarations
Keep these handy and
say them aloud each day!

Attitudes of a De-Stressor

☀ I LEARN FROM THE PAST AND LET IT GO.

☀ I RELEASE RESENTMENTS AND ANGER FOR MY OWN SAKE.

☀ I KNOW WHAT I CAN AND CANNOT CONTROL.

☀ I LET GO OF WHAT I CANNOT CONTROL.

☀ I FOCUS ON WHAT I CAN CONTROL.

☀ I TAKE RESPONSIBILITY FOR MY ACTIONS TODAY.

☀ I INFLUENCE THE FUTURE BY MASTERING MYSELF.

☀ I HAVE THE POWER TO DE-STRESS MY BODY, MIND, EMOTIONS, SPIRIT AND RELATIONSHIPS.

☀ I AM A POWERFUL DE-STRESSOR.

Stand up! Say this aloud with
your hand on your heart. *Feel* the vibration!

Daily Declarations
Keep these handy and
say them aloud each day!

Attitudes of Personal Power

☀ I HAVE THE RIGHT TO MY THOUGHTS.

☀ I HAVE THE RIGHT TO MY FEELINGS.

☀ I HAVE THE RIGHT TO MAKE MY OWN CHOICES.

☀ I AM A UNIQUE INDIVIDUAL AND EQUAL TO OTHERS.

☀ I STATE MY VIEWS AND DESIRES CLEARLY AND CONFIDENTLY.

☀ I CAN AGREE TO DISAGREE.

☀ I TAKE FULL RESPONSIBLITY FOR MY THOUGHTS, FEELINGS AND ACTIONS.

☀ I DO NOT TAKE RESPONSIBILITY FOR THE THOUGHTS, FEELINGS AND ACTIONS OF OTHERS.

☀ I HAVE THE POWER TO BE AND ASSERT WHO I AM IN THE WORLD.

Stand up! Say this aloud with
your hand on your heart. *Feel* the vibration!

Chapter 10
Recommended Resources

Aila's Bookstore
A site for recommended books, CDs and DVDs
http://tinyurl.com/cyygnl

De-Stressing Your Body
Learn about supplements for health by e-mail. Ask your questions about general health, weight management, sleep, energy, allergies, children's health and more....
ailaspeaks@gmail.com

Instructions for safe and fun stretching at
www.stretch.com

Food is a large component of de-stressing and getting the body's natural systems under control. Whole food is the answer to better health. Find recipes, information and classes for healthy eating at www.eatsofeden.com

Article
www.ailaspeaks.com/article-de-stress-body.html

De-Stressing Your Mind
Relaxing Your Body & Mind CD or MP3 **(My gift to you!)**
http://www.ailaspeaks.com/book-bonus-mp3.html

Breaking the Perfection Myth™
http://www.ailaspeaks.com/programs.html

Vision Boards
Article for making a Vision Board
http://www.ailaspeaks.com/article-vision-board.html

Online Vision Board
http://tinyurl.com/afmswv

Articles
www.ailaspeaks.com/article-de-stress-body.html
www.ailaspeaks.com/article-meditation.html
www.ailaspeaks.com/article-to-do-list.html

De-Stressing Your Emotions
See free hugs video at:
www.youtube.com/watch?v=vr3x_RRJdd4
International Free Hug Day is September 10.

Song from *Rising in Love* CD by David Roth
"Don't should on me and I won't should on you"
http://tinyurl.com/cyygnl

Articles
www.ailaspeaks.com/article-emotional-stress.html
www.ailaspeaks.com/article-feast-for-fear.html
www.ailaspeaks.com/article-change.html

Emotional Freedom Techniques (EFT) Resources
Demonstration Video
http://www.youtube.com/watch?v=9l-VDOGqmd4

Free Get Started Package
http://tinyurl.com/cktnyy

DVD Library
http://tinyurl.com/6syqnd

Try It On Everything Movie
http://tinyurl.com/4o3qzp

Tapping Points Reference Sheet (pdf)
http://www.box.net/shared/c9xsc6lhj6

De-Stressing Your Spirit
You Are The Gift   CD or MP3 download
http://www.ailaspeaks.com/guided-meditations.html

What are Your Gifts? (pdf) **(My gift to you!)**
http://www.box.net/shared/cndggtqzso

The Passion Test Book
http://tinyurl.com/q62cv

A Mindfulness Story
http://www.box.net/shared/0llq0pjt1o

Restore Your Vibrations
www.soundsfromsource.com

Articles
www.ailaspeaks.com/article-spiritual-stress.html
www.ailaspeaks.com/article-holiday-stress.html

De-Stressing Your Relationships
Harville Hendrix
Getting the Love You Want
Keeping the Love You Find
In Aila's Bookstore: http://tinyurl.com/cyygnl

Paul & Layne Cutright
You're Never Upset for the Reason You Think
http://tinyurl.com/c93hxd

Articles
www.ailaspeaks.com/article-relationship-stress.html

This Resource List is updated continuously.
If you find resources you like, let us know at:
ailaspeaks@gmail.com

Shop for Additional Resources from
LifeQuest International, LLC and Aila Accad, RN
www.AilaSpeaks.com

BOOKS
Wake Up, Live the Life You Love: In the Now (2009)
Little Seed Publishing

PROGRAMS TO INSPIRE & TRANSFORM
De-stress & leadership for business, nurses and schools
Transform individual lives and work environments for happiness, health & productivity

The De-Stress ToolBox™
Four DVDs and Action Guide
To get rid of stress finally! Learn the only cause of all stress and four tools to handle stress quickly in any situation

Breaking the Perfection Myth™
A model for freedom, peace and self-esteem

Leaving the Well™
An experiential model for recovery from addiction, depression and spiritual distress

Weight No More TeleCoaching Program™
A coaching program for permanent weight release.

GUIDED MEDITATIONS ~ VOLUME ONE
A six-CD or MP3 set with original meditations and music compositions
Includes Relaxing Your Body & Mind, Creating Your Sacred Space, Accessing Your Inner Wisdom, Creating Your Energy Shield, Energizing Your Life and You Are the Gift.

DE-STRESS COACHING

You have access to a master guide who provides the support, tools and techniques learned from 40 years on the inner journey and teaches them to you for complete self-mastery. Individual and group coaching by phone.

WOMEN'S RETREATS

Attend a retreat with others at Aila's Retreat Center or invite Aila to plan a retreat for your group or to celebrate a special life transition.

NEWSLETTER

De-Stress Tips and News
Sign up free at ailaspeaks.com

About the Author

With 40 years of education and experience in the areas of personal and interpersonal growth, Aila Accad synthesizes huge amounts of information into simple principles and effective tools that everyone can use!

Aila is a registered nurse, with bachelor's and master's degrees in Nursing. She is a Certified Well-Being Coach, EFT Advanced Practitioner, Reiki Master and founder of LifeQuest International, LLC, which specializes in unique self-growth techniques that produce profound and lasting results.

People who attend Aila's life-changing seminars call them "powerful," "inspiring" and "fun." Known as the "De-Stress Expert," Aila has written articles for research journals and books.

She is past president of the West Virginia Nurses Association, past board member of the Charleston Area Chamber of Commerce, recipient of Business Woman of the Year Award and designated Distinguished Toastmaster by Toastmasters International. Her biography appears in Who's Who in American Nursing and Who's Who of Women Executives.

Aila lives in Charleston, WV, surrounded by nature's beauty and bounty.

Contact her at ailaspeaks.com.